Following Sea

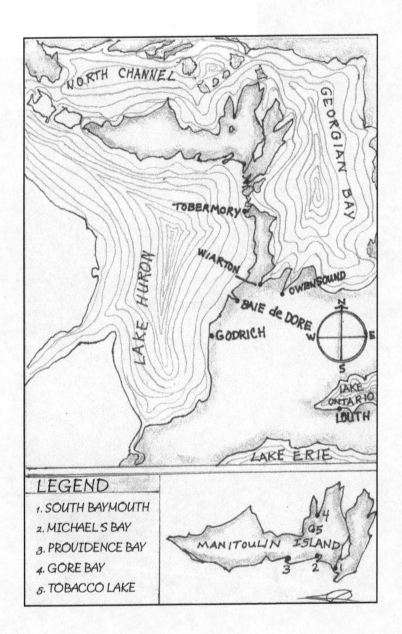

NORTH CHANNEL

GEORGIAN BAY

TOBERMORY

WIARTON

OWEN SOUND

BAIE de DORE

LAKE HURON

GODRICH

N
W   E
S

LAKE ONTARIO
LOUTH

LAKE ERIE

LEGEND
1. SOUTH BAYMOUTH
2. MICHAEL'S BAY
3. PROVIDENCE BAY
4. GORE BAY
5. TOBACCO LAKE

MANITOULIN ISLAND

For Sheila — with all best wishes + may your seas be following

Following Sea

by Lauren Carter

Lauren Carter

TURNSTONE PRESS

Turnstone Press
Artspace Building
206-100 Arthur Street
Winnipeg, MB
R3B 1H3 Canada
www.TurnstonePress.com

Turnstone Press gratefully acknowledges the assistance of the Canada Council for the Arts, the Manitoba Arts Council, the Government of Canada through the Canada Book Fund, and the Province of Manitoba through the Book Publishing Tax Credit and the Book Publisher Marketing Assistance Program.

Cover image *Openings* and hand drawn map illustration by Laura Carter

Printed and bound in Canada.

Library and Archives Canada Cataloguing in Publication

Title: Following sea / Lauren Carter.

Names: Carter, Lauren, 1972- author.

Description: Poems.

Identifiers: Canadiana (print) 20189067632 | Canadiana (ebook) 20189067640 | ISBN 9780888016577 (softcover) | ISBN 9780888016584 (EPUB) | ISBN 9780888016591 (Kindle) | ISBN 9780888016607 (PDF)
Classification: LCC PS8605.A863 F65 2019 | DDC C811/.6—dc23

MANITOBA ARTS COUNCIL
CONSEIL DES ARTS DU MANITOBA

Canada Council Conseil des arts
for the Arts du Canada

Funded by the Government of Canada
Financé par le gouvernement du Canada

Canada

Manitoba

MIX
Paper from
responsible sources
FSC® C004071

ANCIENT FOREST ™
FRIENDLY

For Clive 'Scott' Chisholm (1936–2007),

Laura Alderson Chisholm (1902–1980),

and for Jason.

I swim toward you
In a stream that carries
A hook of memory, bait
Of flung down years,

Its colour singing.

—Clive 'Scott' Chisholm

Contents

Historian / 5

Following Sea

Michael's Bay / 9
Baie du Doré / 11
Prayer / 13
Tobacco Lake / 15
Island Clearances / 17
Walking Glen Affric (2016) / 24
Following Sea / 25
Ghost / 28

Migration

Louth (1851) / 33
Home (1854) / 35
Passage (1854) / 36
Clearing the Land (1856) / 37
Starvation Year (1858-59) / 38
Swamp Fire (1862) / 41
Migration (1868) / 42
Walker's Point, Manitoulin
    Island (1868) / 45
Blacksmith (1871) / 47
The Lighthouse (1879) / 49

Homecoming

Georgian Bay / 53
Homecoming (2010) / 55
The Bard / 56
Preserved / 58
Consumption / 59
Crossing the Bay / 62
Notes from Proceedings of
     Medical Board at Discharge
     Depot: A Found Poem / 64
Heartbreak / 66
Fourteen Years / 68

Barren

Barren / 73
Destroying the Evidence
     (September) / 75
October / 76
Squall (November) / 77
December / 78
Farmer's Wife (January) / 80
February / 81
Homestead (March) / 82
Maypole / 83
Test / 85
Moth / 86
Remains / 87

Mother's Day

Ticks   / 91
For History   / 93
Boundaries   / 95
Beacons   / 97
Granadilla   / 99
Leeches   / 100
Excavation   / 101
Guardian   / 103
Mother's Day   / 104
Spring   / 106

Acknowledgements   / 108

Following Sea

A following sea:

A sea that is moving in the same direction
as the heading of the boat

Historian

Awake, in thick night
on the second storey, the dog
a shadow in the window
well, my nightmare spreads open
into now.

Something I can taste, touch,
and smell like the scent of spent
copper beneath the sheets.

How can it be that life
is always wasted, a ceremony
spreading salt into the soil every
twenty-eight days?

All I can do is peer
back: flash through microfiche,
flip through worn ledgers, my lead
tip skimming lines fine as the blue

beneath thin skin of the wrist,
searching columns of surnames
fat as sticks, hunting
for the familiar:

> *John Willson Chisholm (1823–1900),*
> *wife Margaret Patterson (1824–1891)*

the ones who went north, into wild
woods, onto island,
who followed the ridge
of stone, boney as a fetal

spine, until I find
them: pressed
between pages, those sudden
cursive blooms.

*

I look backwards
because the future
is too hard to bear: another
bitter winter, so many
empty snares.

Following Sea

Michael's Bay

Yellow grass grows
to dirt edge of stone

cellars. Shadows lit
by broken glass.

Monarchs drift
like the hems of long

dresses, over milkweeds'
fleshy heads.

Ladders of lathe
leading nowhere, grown

into the river's
mud bank, a midden

that remains from this once
busy place called home.

* * *

Earlier, we walked
into the cedar's fragrant

gloom. It's assumed,
our guide said, that this

is where they are: bones
hidden in a heap of soil

within a snake-fenced
square, no stone

to hold their names.

Baie du Doré

West, we drive,
away from any land
we know, into valleys
carved by the river
you stand within,
threading flat hooks
again and again.

I leave you there,
waist deep in cold
current, and drive
to the lake to look
for signs of stone
homes in the sand
near the nuclear
power plant,

hunting the remains
of the swamp
fire that emptied
their shanties, turned
log homes to embers
and ash, excised
the town
where my people
once lived.

But there's nothing
now, land
claimed by wind
turbines, farms
for sale, schoolhouses
holding wreckage
in their yards.

When the street
dead-ends at the lake, I sit
for a spell, staring out
at blind horizon,
the past as hidden
as the future

you are searching, sifting
through rivers, seeking
other forms.

Prayer

Bits of magic, my uncle
prescribes: shells

and stones and bark
from the leaning spruce. In a cabin,

by the light of a glass lantern,
the gifts come: a clam shell

crowded with pebbles, a yellow rock
hollowed at its core. With warm

hands damp from dishes, my mother
and aunt encircle us, bend

with the words they say, prayers
to request our long-sought

blessing of a baby. Together,
we build a temple

where a family
holds tight: my uncle

askew on the hard, red chair,
my sister, sunk into silence.

Dark night on the blurry
window panes, that wider

world, impossible
to see.

Tobacco Lake

My mother's wrinkled hands
rub soap into my uncle's hair,
reach for him as he tips
into the lake.

Together, they struggle
in this place that once
was their playground, my mother
crawling across the ribbed,
sandy bottom like a crab, my uncle
planning mischief.

Crouched, nearby, I dig
shells out of the mud
and watch them, silhouetted
by the dropping sun. Two old
people wrapped in a silence far
from my breathing, in a place
I have not learned.

Together, they stumble
in smaller footprints while I listen
to my breath counting
time, to the laughter
of my nephews nearby.

Later, for the youngest boy,
my uncle describes the lake's
sea monster, his eyes
catching the light
of an early moon as he sits
on the splintered dock, leaning
toward its edge.

My mother holds her brother
upright as my nephew gazes
out, searching for the creature's distant
shape, for its scaled back breaking
the water's quiet skin.

Island Clearances

This land like a mirror turns you inward

                —Gwendolyn MacEwen

I.

Sunset. The thinnest pink
wash from the hump of the hill

and in blurred woods
beside the car, I see a lynx,

running, racing
alongside, that giant

blonde cat coming clear
only to me. My brother

and sister in the back
seat, my parents

up front, pushing on
into night in the middle

of the island.

II.
Manitoulin Island, where light
is fine-boned, water teal

of the tropics or, in brown
Tobacco Lake, as warm.

I did not know, not
then, as a child, or later

in the inflatable raft
where I paddled pale

hands around the stone-
shelved shore of Lake

Manitou, about the few
short years between island

home of Anishinaabe
and my people docking

there to live, packing fish
into barrels, like looted

silver, sold.

III.
Only a century
and a half since my family set

foot on that shore, began
thickening their blood

with limestone
silt. So soon, yet it's in

me, the way the pocked
rock of Misery Bay feels

underfoot, how the hard
sand collapses in your hands

on the long,
wet crawl to horizon.

Autumn wind in Tehkummah
pulling light through golden

grass, a spiral of swallows
over dark water at dusk, sandhills

calling into quiet.

IV.
In the 1860s, cold
silence hung over island

dwellings as my ancestors
crawled up the Indian

Peninsula, crossed over
black opal of bay.

Three generations
after exile

from the Highlands,
the scent of Scots

pine caught like a dream
in the dust of felled

cedar, white pine wide
as the river where salmon

stitch a lineage
inside the liquid

weave. In the autumn,
of 1863, a group

of Anishinaabe
tried to stop the white

surveyors arriving
onshore. They were there

to count the trout, tally
stone and trees, to see

if the soil
could be turned.

V.
My great-great-grandfather
built a lighthouse

to mark
the tallow-thick mist

of Michael's Bay
where the mill

slivered trees,
fat as fourteen feet

in girth,
into thousands

of shingles
for settler homes.

VI.
Cedar snake
fences fallen in stone-

clotted fields. Soil stripped
from the bedrock

we walk before leaving
by ferry, crossing big water

back home.

Walking Glen Affric (2016)

On the final morning, it rained. A sleet of silver
from distant domes, dampening the thick mist
that clouded the last twelve miles of trail.

Through this, we walked, along a footpath scratched
in granite, tiled with scrambled shale, water
streaming into the valley far below. Down

in the depths of the darkest peat, the long,
shimmering thread of a loch, looping
the footprints of four rock walls, built

in a distant past by bodies flushed with the same
bright blood as mine. My kin, the ancestors
I'd crossed an ocean to see. But as we walked,

pushed for an opening in the curtain of rain,
all that remained was stone, tumbled loose, heaped
into cairns where my footsteps soon would fade.

* Glen Affric is a glen in the Scottish Highlands which was
part of the Clan Chisholm lands from the 15th to the mid-19th
century.

Following Sea

The weather turns the world
to cloud, water painted in slate

as I keep my eyes aimed ahead,
Wiarton vanishing like a sailor's

illusion of land. Yesterday,
in the library, I searched for traces

of my family, found my uncle's
book on the shelf. All morning,

the cemetery
tugged at me, but I didn't go.

Stayed inside and counted
names, sifted notations,

ran my finger down death
notices and photocopied script.

My great-great-grandparents
gazed out at me, in a blur of black

and white, their strangers'
faces reflecting mine.

I don't know what I wanted.

To walk by my grandmother's
house, see the lopsided barn

still standing, her fruit trees
heavy with cherries. To enter

her yellow kitchen, smell
the oil stove, the musty

hollow of the root cellar
where she kept our crayon

bucket and her canned
pear preserves.

But this town is empty
now, no one left but strange

cousins who don't know me
like she did.

On Division Street,
around the corner from her house,

we bought smoked trout,
carried it back to the boat. Roped

off White Cloud Island, we ate
the last before sailing for home,

wide swells following, flattened
to tables, crowded with ghosts.

Ghost

Before dawn had burned
the ice off the night, Margaret

stirred ashes, moved stiff limbs
to pioneer tasks: cooked meat

in the heat of the hearth,
strung sheets of apple to dry,

wrapped wicks in tallow until inches
were built, bunched nettles to hang

from the rafters for tea. It's she
who knew how to live

through hard things, bury
a son and keep on, days

spinning to winter
when the fire gathered

her children, girls working
needles, careful stitches

to count the days.

* * *

Tea tastes of bitter pith, costs
more money than sense.

I lay hands on hot
mug and move back to bed,

take stock of cold soil, sift hands
through this clutter of tasks.

Migration

Louth (1851)

All around them are rivers
tumbling from fossilled stone.

Ships nudge their openings,
white sails falling
like the wings of a hawk
as she watches
her husband's handiwork:

barrels built of corseted
oak, fat with stone
fruit, salted fish, straddled
up the gangplank.

She did not know
it wouldn't last.
Not in those young
days, first babies
born close, the crowded,
wet litter of a cat.

She thought they could stay
with family, walk well-
trammelled paths beat
into the earth, for always.

But north they'd go, where
there was nothing.

Trees fat as castles.

A stony, grey shore.

Home (1854)

Their new home, a mark
on the map, the ink
of vast water
spotted by stains.

John's finger,
floating, above.

At night, the fire
pulls the world
in close.

Her parents, their past,
erased in flickering
edges, pine sap popping
like the crack
of cold glass.

It's a relief to see
the lake: dome of sky

over slate, white
script of waves
like a letter
sent from home.

Passage (1854)

In Goderich, the boat
is a disappointment.

A dug-out canoe quickly
crowded with all of their things.

The baby, close as a burr
on her breast, the boys struck
silent by expanse.

The oars cut through calm
water, rounding a point
marked by pin-prick
of light and then, they were left

on the beach, the hem
of her dress wicking the lake.

Clearing the Land (1856)

Fire burns a warp
of brush.

Scrub softened to dust
to make fields
between the weft
of rock.

Each day, a new
scratch, pink gash
etched on forearm, face, scribbled
like language, the symbols
with which
to knit a sock.

They are trying to unweave
this woodland, spin it
into something new:

what she remembers
of the land
back home: embroidered
gardens, counted
rows, an arithmetic
of orchard trees.

Starvation Year (1858–59)

I.
In the pewter of the dinner
hour they do not eat fresh
meat.

Only shards of salt fish,
nightly revived to their former,
slippery selves.

The last of the corn
meal turned to crust, coffee
brewed from sooty

peas, apple
barrels emptied.

II.
Come February, no one knows
how long it's been, how many
days or weeks.

In the forest, her footsteps
shatter the snow
and like every
other animal, her breath

is made material, hovering
over her head like prayer.

III.
In spring, the land is full
of wraiths, eyes larger

than the lake's slow
spread of blue.

Released, the earth sends
sweet leeks
and cow cabbage,
fiddleheads that loosen
their grip

in the pot, but nothing
that gives weight
to the bowl.

IV.
At last, the boats come,
carrying deliverance:

grain and corn and flour
as funds for clearing
the Saugeen Road.

With bones like stones in loose
sand, they start again: gathering,

baking, burying seeds
to stack the root
cellar full, to take them through

to December, when they'll butcher
the pigs, blood
on the snow

like the berries
of bittersweet woven
to wreaths on their doors.

Swamp Fire (1862)

Black trees buckled
in an odd alphabet, still
smouldering.

Smoke stings her eyes, coals
crushed underfoot
like acorn caps
in autumn.

What was here, gone,
transformed to a new
geography, an empty map.

Their house, a fallen
effort, its embers soldering
her leaden skirts.

Migration (1868)

I.
Five years by then
in Owen Sound. Six
children. A shop
at Boyd's Wharf
where the schooners
and steamers
slid in, cutting

calm water to sell
the fish that frothed
in the shallows
offshore, and carry
passengers south
to Meaford.

In John's eyes
every boat
took them with it.

II.
She belongs
to what she left
behind: black char
of the village, burned
to the ground, Richard,
fourth son, buried
back there.

III.
The walls of close
forest rebuilt
her past, those ribbons

of water that tumble
from stone, soft
grit on her fingers

like ash as she follows
the Sydenham River
from town, hunting red

birthroot in the rust-
coloured beds
of last year.

IV.
I don't know
why John had to go
so far from escarpment's
strong spine, but after

John Jr. married
his Margaret, they left,
embarked the boat
once again.

Fish a silver shelf
far below, gulls grey
shadows in sun.

Like pollen, the children
drifted the deck
as the harbour

fell farther, shrank
back.

Walker's Point, Manitoulin Island (1868)

Like relocated animals
looking for a ready den,
they were dropped ashore again

at an outpost between wild
sea and wilderness.

The lake sand swallowed
their soles as if begging
them to stay and John
began building

on the limestone flat
where the wood shop
would be.

It wasn't what she'd hoped—
sons toiling within the great
water's dream, daughters

marrying mill workers,
the sharp stench
of fish spoiling the air.

But it was the life
that came.

She gathered the days
and ordered them.

Made jam from ruby
fruit in blackened
clearings, braided the earth
in plaits of green.

Blacksmith (1871)

Then, they lived
beside the blacksmith,

his geyser of sparks.
In winter, the only colour:

that red hot shoe
hissing into the bucket

of blood.
John and the men

talked while he worked,
his fingertips marked with scars

like stars, like a tally
in chalk.

They did not enter,
the women.

Those fires
burned only for men,

for the hard things
that were required: nails

and barrel hoops, horse
shoes, hammered

blades. Their own iron
was internal.

Formed from many
babies, and missed souls,

those fissures
veined in ore.

The Lighthouse (1879)

In Michael's Bay,
the air was cluttered
with a fine, sweet
dust, like the mist
their lighthouse lit,
forty feet
above the lake.

From the keeper's
house, the last
girl left—Jane,
marrying
into the Snows—

while the boys
stayed close, carried
coal, helped to turn
the heavy lens.

Like a return
to the land they'd left,
John planted plums
in the shallow,
stony soil,

and all summer
she leaned
into the shifting
wind, waiting

to taste the sweetness
surrounding bitter pits
while he lit
the constant lantern
against the water's
darkest edge.

Homecoming

Georgian Bay

Out here, only
horizon. A meniscus

of emptiness,
air and water.

Under the width
of unfurled swells,

diving down, you'd find
fathoms, 540 feet deep.

The bones of wrecks:
the *Northern Belle*,

the *Waubuno*, the *Asia*
which took all but two

survivors, a hundred
and more souls

swallowed in a quick,
gulping turn

of the weather.
Timbers and scaled

iron scattered
over a secret

terrain, the remains
of ancient waterfalls,

eight thousand
years old, stilled

in silent depths.

Homecoming (2010)
(for my mother)

Wind blows from the great bay
to boreal, churning the skin
of the silted lake where your brother
dissolved like salt two summers ago.

I know what you are looking for:
the father who died when you had just turned
thirteen, the barber shop where he shaved
farmers and fishermen before
you were born. The bones

of your life set
in a single place, so you follow
the highway north
into white quartz
hills and out into the harvest,
into autumn on the island:

lace flowers of the wild
carrot closed like cinched
purses, a blurred letter
of geese overhead, the blood

red berries eaten by jays, those heavy
apples, dropping.

The Bard
(for Unc)

Like a road sign at a dusty
island intersection, a pause

in the story, and we look east
and west over peaches-and-cream

corn cooked for his homecoming,
wondering which way he'll turn.

His stories took us places
he knew we'd never been,

his Ontario kin, settled so close
to home while he had roamed

all the way to Death
Valley, striding over white heat

in worn sneakers. That
is what killed him. That

and the childhood
fever that weakened

his heart, the slow
trounce of a stroke

so he couldn't even go
to the bathroom by himself,

this man who'd disappear
for months, sailing the slow

grasslands of Nebraska, hiking
stone roads in Spain. But even

at his weakest, eased
to the table's mooring

for a saucer of pills, dribbling
tea down his shirt, he remained

the storyteller, the bard,
a single finger standing

in silent exposition long after
he'd fallen to sleep.

Preserved

At the edge
of Providence
Bay, my great-grandmother,
       Mary Lueza Gardner Chisholm (1872–1904)
is buried in the ground
like an artifact, a seed
from a desert urn
that could still sprout
a fresh green heart.

This is the story
that my uncle told,
when I was a child
in the cemetery
under red pines
shrieking in the wind
off the bay: how she lay
as if asleep, her body
preserved in sandy soil,
hands cupped over clavicle
in the quiet coffin's space

so I imagined
digging her up, witnessing
the resemblance,
shaking her awake.

Consumption
(for John Chisholm, 1893–1914)

I.
There are others here like him,
their coughing
calls in a strange aviary.

Outside, on the grass
sloping down
to the lake, they stretch
arms out in unison, reach

faces to feet and rise,
in formation,
a flock flying south
every fall. Behind,

the sanitarium, white
like marble
against the blue.

II.
In the afternoon,
he takes to bed,
tucks his moulting
feathers, picks
up a pen
with the bones
of his hand
to scratch
a note, a bird
spitting shells,
having eaten
the seed: *I know*
I won't
come home.

III.
Back home, fields
coated in cold, diamond
down, an autumn wind pushing
light from the bay. Big
water, wide swells,
not small like this lake
he walks so slowly to see.

Its far shore a soot
scribble of obvious truth.

IV.
His mother's body
where she was buried:

under pines too tall
for his eyes, how the sand
slid back
into her open grave,
the earth
refusing to accept her.

V.
Those valleys he wandered
within, dragging nets to catch
that limitless
current of whitefish.

Mist so thick all they could do
was hold still as if swaddled,
and wait for shore to come clear.

His lungs alight
like a man underwater
holding tight
to his pocket of air.

Crossing the Bay
(for Grace Chisholm, 1901–1926)

At sixteen, in shoes
crowded by crab grass

and Queen Anne's Lace, Grace
wed her first cousin, the bad

seed, the one they called
Black Jack.

In Manitowaning, to hide
their relation, she recorded

her surname as Johnson,
not incorrectly,

for her father, Walter
Wilson, was the son of John.

I wonder if that was her
idea and if she also chose

to cross the big water
to Thessalon where she bore

five children in deep
woods before dying,

days ahead of the returning
birds: rheumatic fever,

an inflammation
of the inner lining of the heart.

Notes from Proceedings of Medical Board at
Discharge Depot: A Found Poem
(for Herman Walter "Duff" Chisholm, 1898-1955)

I.
Six months in trenches.

Pleurisy April 1917.

Pneumonia
at the same time.

First noticed swelling
of ankles and face

Jan. 1917. Given
M and D.

He now complains
of pain

in the back
dizziness, shortness

of breath. In cloudy
and stormy

weather headache
comes on. This man

has pallor, puffiness
of face. Heart enlarged

outside of nipple line, sounds
accentuated

II.
Patient
extremely nervous.

Complains
of restlessness

and insomnia. Tremors
of fingers. Knee

jerks markedly
and muscular

twitching
on the slightest

stimulus

Heartbreak

I.
Still water, mirrored
doldrums—what the blood
becomes in my grandfather's
veins, after a doctor
gave him too much digitalis
to treat the first
of ten heart attacks
in 1936.

Slowed, like swells
thickening to slush,
his blood left his limbs,
his skin flushing blue, a rot

my grandmother witnessed
before his leg was lost,
cut away beneath the knee.

II.
Fourteen years later, my child-
mother smiles for a photograph,

her face soft, having learned
to be still on the rough
chop of their lives.

Cane propped
against a wooden leg
hidden by the hollow
drape of his trousers.

To the living
shin she clings, anchoring

him, her own heart
holding a child's steady
pace, four years
before it will break.

Fourteen Years

The first winter, they lived
on the island, where my grandfather
wanted to stay. Storms
building snow against the outer

world while they sewed
a quilt, heavy as a lead
apron laid over the body
when looking within.

By spring, my grandmother
needed to leave, her loneliness
floating them west by ferry
to family

on the peninsula. The island
a sliver of shale, a shrinking
dark door, blocked
by rough waves, bad weather.

Wiarton was my grandmother's
home, heart of a web
of seven siblings raised
as her own

after uterine cancer killed
their mother, aged thirty-one.
Her father found work
as a flour miller, while she, the eldest

living girl, left
school, having finished
grade four.
Her sisters, surrogate

children, grew to women
who bore the infants her own body
refused, dreams
dampened to dark

clots month after month,
until one summer, she thought
she'd caught the flu,
fourteen years

after that long island winter,
newly wed, spent
within the close,
heavy weight of the bed.

Barren

Barren

You are still in the dream world.

I take down notes with twitching
fingers as the morning

crowns, a pearly blue.
It is the colour of my pyjama top.

It is the colour of my first
bedroom

away from home. In the night,
I dreamt I had been pregnant

but lost the baby. My mother
and sister and I strained

to remember: Where
had it gone?

Was it a boy or a girl?

The daytime is so much
more practical, every answer

available on the Internet, all
the truths spelled out—the outside

temperature, the cost
to mail a parcel to Japan,

the perfect recipe
for chicken paprikash—but

it can't tell me this:
where did my future go, why

is my body a bone
dry field that only dust

will know.

Destroying the Evidence (September)

I do not have a red tent,
a bamboo hut, or several sisters,
pressing into my pain. Instead,
I am alone. In secret,

I gather my blood
in bowls, erase it
from being, mute
it with the toilet's flush.

Scrub the sheets, wipe
the white
tile floor, ensure
there are no marks.

Soundless, these cycles
happen, this monthly
dirge. Hidden

in the crimson glare
where no one ever goes.

October

The animal
doesn't want me.

I am too bitter,
too stale.

My skin doesn't crackle
enough, is pale.

The quiet morning
draws clouds
across its lap
like laying
a napkin
before a meal.

I ask again
for it to eat
me, swallow
me whole,

but its stomach
is too small
for the heavy course
it would endure.

Squall (November)

All night the house stood
in the wind.

Gate slamming the beast's
arrival, over
and over again.

A sailor's wife, I stare
out into the gale, having
never caught a glimpse
of you, beyond
my marriage
day.

You disappeared

like ash caught
in the clutch
of a gust: a ribcage
carved out of air,
slow weave of hair,
swallowed
by the squall
deep inside its lair.

December

Gifts pile by our bed
like bricks, each difficult
to break. I chisel
until they crumble and cup
red dust in my hand.

At night we breathe
it in and the tiny
diamonds make our dreams.

But I am tired
of sleep, those ice
doors, the dammed
streams, all these brittle
days piled like a pyre, waiting
to ignite.

Outside, people stroll
the sidewalks, pointed
in one of two
directions, uptown
or down, bright
bags hanging
from their mittened
hands.

Their eyes are grey
like the landscape, their eyes
are grey like the skin
of the sky, arched over

the mourning
doves perched frozen
on the line.

Farmer's Wife (January)

From bedroom
to kitchen, I inch.

One hand
on the rope, avoiding

outside slope
of snow. Winter

cracking the glass
with a storm

I cannot enter.

Nothing to care for.

No creatures to feed
at the end of long

struggle, hands
hoisting hot bodies, heart

pressed to soft hide.

February

Two weeks past the family day
and we have eaten nothing. Anorexic-

slim, we are reductions of our plump,
pink selves. Our bones gather

in the night, ladders
to each other under the red,

red quilt. This is purity,
this giving up, this standing

back from the steep face of stone
showing scenes from our lives.

We are familiars: bound by geology
of ice, the cold like a father

come home from the war.

Homestead (March)

This is all
we have: so little

to eat, each day
the drone

of an emptying
hive, that perfect

sweetness
pocketed

away, held
in cells,

unreachable.

Maypole

All over the house
fires flare in damp ashes.

In the corner
of the kitchen,

in my underwear
drawer, within the cellar's

rubble walls.
They draw me close,

like ghosts flickering
on the edges, asking

me to feed them,
even as I fold them

into dark pleats
of sleep. They burn

through that. They burn
through everything.

In the morning, my skin
is singed

and all I remember
are blue forks

of flame, the spinning,
ecstatic dance.

Test

Blue bleeds
into early morning:
plus sign, elusive
equation, after seven
years, the test
taken and passed.

At the party
for my nephew's
birthday, we give
a grain of rice,
call it cousin.

My sister screams
with glee, my
mother's eyes hover
on my plate in a way
I've never seen
her watching.

Before the week
is out, she will buy
us furniture: a wooden
rocker, a cradle

swinging empty
from its frame.

Moth

I sat on the rock slope for over
an hour, watching the flutter
of a moth.

The wings an ordinary
colour of overcast sky

but when they opened:
purple and orange
like a fire's deepest roots.

With legs like filament,
it stood on my finger, stayed

while I wondered about its species,
its hidden, human name, felt a flood

in my heart, rushing, full. The world
right then, remarkable: your life

in my body, your name,
long-chosen. Your wings,

already opening, although
we did not know.

Remains

The nurse left us in the glass
room and closed the door

as the police wrestled
with a man spewing vomit

across the clean tile floor.
Through the black

grid of the window, we watched,
joking about zombies,

planning our escape.
In the waiting room I had already turned

you out, body labouring
over a crimson slip that fell

into the toilet, sank down
like a leech. The remains

of you, that still,
dead centre of who

you would have been.

Mother's Day

Ticks

The first spring harvest
at the writing retreat
is ticks, those blind
infants crawling up
out of grass
along the trail
of flesh to fasten like blown
flakes of seed.

In my room, I strip
in front of the full-length
mirror, twist calves and turn
to cup the round
white orb of each plump
buttock, blue-veined
breasts hoisted
to peer
into the shadowy
corners of the barren
body I avoid.

Out in the fields,
before the black
army came,
I had been crying,

facing again the old
pain that thrusts its head

down deep and feeds,
that tells me I am dust
and leaves.

For History

I have nothing to give
you, history. Only words
on pages that might
or might not rot.

You cannot have
my blood, mixed
in the veins
of my great-great-
great-great-great-
grandparents
who crossed
an ocean as children
in the hold of a ship,

so many deaths at sea
that the captain
fled the authorities
in the New York port.

It's a miracle I am
even here.

My grandfather, a boy
soldier in the trenches,
my mother, a toddler,
with meningitis,

my father, a farm boy,
surviving his own antics,
the propulsion
of an exploding glass
jar, a toy he'd built himself.

It's simple, really, the cold
fact: my own miracle
did not come to pass.

History, you planted
a single, faulty seed,
husk too hard,
tender sprout
a green wither.

You cannot have
my blood.

Boundaries

At the house of the artist,
silence like a bell jar.

Outside the back door, a river
running orange from cedar roots.

Past that, the fields, where one
afternoon, movement marked

the minutes of the sun's slow
arc and through binoculars

I saw a coyote, far off,
safe from the imposition

of humans, pouncing
on its hidden prey.

Even I hadn't walked
that far, to the high wall

of the wood where bears
wander, the painter had warned

in a worried hush,
as if speaking of a witch

in a fairy tale, who might exit
her dark world to snatch

what she needs
from the light.

Beacons

These slow few seconds of dawn
like promises made, maintained,

like the vows we've been repeating
since October when we sat
on the side of a highway
and watched the forest learn
to let go.

Months since then, growing
colder.

In the evening, as the pale
day fades away, we kindle
our fires, build blue

and amber against a colourless
winter, remind each other
of the coming
of the light: a return

to that worn path
we walked last autumn
where we stopped

to admire the mushrooms,
their fluorescent bodies glowing
in beds of dead

leaves, bitterness sweetened
by the beauty of their dress.

Granadilla

Standing in the kitchen with feet cold
we hold the fruit from Columbia
like the memory of an earlier day
we are still trying to get right.

We haven't seen one before—bright
as a tangerine until its carapace
splits open under the knife

and inside the small sun is colour
like that early one: a lake of purple
ice, spotted with startling darkness.

It is surprising, this exploration,
in a kitchen not yet warm after two
days away, where we eat the fruit,

enjoy the crunch of black seed,
the subtle sweet taste,
even if it isn't
what we are expecting:

that small, hot heaven, melting
an opening
in early winter, standing in
for something else.

Leeches

Beneath jack pine, beside
blueberries, they rush
to us, smelling what we have
to offer. Our darkness
is what they're after: those rivers

that flow through invisible
thickets, the black
as it brightens to red. In Secret

Bay, granite lines a lake
lit orange from sunken
cedar and when your white
skin flashes free, I see
how your instep is suckled
by a single, large leech,
the clots of her hundred babies.

You do not scream.
Like a dancer, you extend
your foot, ask me for my help.

Calmly, I sprinkle salt and watch
as they curl away, drop down
and disappear inside the lake's decay.

Excavation

The grey days are over
but still the serpent

stays inside, cooling its belly
on the stone of my rib.

I poke it with a worn
stick and it writhes,

its body spelling shapes
of past mistakes.

Where will I go
from here, the snake

gaining strength
in the gloom.

Each day a recounting
of absence, the calendar

cold but not yet
covered in snow,

like limestone revealing
the clutter of eons:

hollow bone
of vertebrae, a wing

written into the rock,
worn evidence

of what endures.

Guardian

That morning, we left
the house with the dog,
ducked under a spider
web we wouldn't destroy.

I can't remember deciding,
only that it was done,

after eight years our taste
gone for the bitter
Chinese teas that altered
every week.

In the driveway, I slid
my hand into yours,
and we turned north,
led by the leash, startled

by a sudden shadow that lifted
our eyes to the wide reach
of an owl's broad wings.

Its yellow gaze met mine.

I felt it take the lead.

Mother's Day

On Mother's Day, we walk
into the fields from the writing

retreat. Six poets crossing
blonde stubble over rubbled earth, the rattle

of stalks like strengthened verbs.
Down in the valley, a river twists

in wide arcs, its skin drawing in
the last light and the talk

turns to pregnancy, how it can act
as a tonic for cramps.

But I don't care
because I'm there, my eyes

savouring the smallest
detail: the bright white

of a horse on the rise, the smudge
of a moulting coyote trailing her trio

of pups. All this life, its many
variations: the wind

wrestling the flats, rustling
a patch of pale prairie crocus

under a sky spread vermilion
red while we ease

into silence, the weaving
of so many threads.

Spring

We came to this place
voluntarily, our belongings
packed into boxes, stacked
in the truck like a puzzle
of our lives.

Along the Superior highway,
before we broke out
into prairie, the cat sat
on my lap, watched the blue
and black miles move by
like meditation, our past
slowly sliding away.

Up north, the river is a moat
between us and deep boreal, barren
lands two days' distance by train.

Here, we find
new wilderness,

trudge through the snow
toward dawn with the dog,
each morning's colour
saturating the east.

All we know
right now is winter,
not yet the spring—

seventeen hours of sunlight,
shining pods of white
pelicans, drifting like angels
up over the plains.

Acknowledgements

This collection has been in the works for over a decade. Some of the poems first appeared in *FreeFall*, *The Broken City*, the *Winnipeg Free Press*, and *Room*. An earlier version of "Island Clearances" won the 2014 *Room* Poetry Contest and a selection from the manuscript was long-listed as "Migration" for the CBC Poetry Prize. Sincere thanks to the editors and judges who saw their merit. The work was also carried forward with financial assistance from the Ontario Arts Council and the Manitoba Arts Council, for which I'm very grateful.

The line from Gwendolyn MacEwen's poem "Dark Pines Under Water" is used with the permission of David MacKinnon (the estate of Gwendolyn MacEwen) and the line from Scott Chisholm's poem "Only the Best Line Holds," which originally appeared in his chapbook, *Desperate Affections*, published by State Street Press, is used with the permission of Linda Chisholm (the estate of Scott Chisholm).

Early poems were helped by Dionne Brand and the fine poets in my University of Guelph MFA poetry seminar; Elizabeth Philips provided astute notes and feedback on a couple of them. Allan Briesmaster read and offered thoughts on the poem "Following Sea," while Lorri Neilsen Glenn read the full manuscript and gave valuable feedback and support during her time as The Pas Writer-in-Residence. I'm deeply grateful for Jan Zwicky's insightful questions and comments during the Spring 2014 Sage Hill Poetry Colloquium. My thanks and an affectionate shout-out to the other poets in attendance during those magical two weeks: Laurie D. Graham, Micheline Maylor, Joan Shillington, Basma Kavanagh, Alex Pierce, Margo Wheaton, and Deanna Young. I am also thankful for the support and friendship of my Manitoba writing crew: Erna Buffie, Ariel Gordon, Sally Ito, Donna Besel, and Sue Sorenson, in particular.

Alice Major, my editor, provided careful reading and valuable questions and suggestions which helped me see the forest for the trees, so to speak, and trim the snags. Thank you! Thanks, too, to Sharon, Jamis, Melissa, and Sarah at Turnstone Press.

My appreciation also goes out to the many important archives that allowed me to inch towards an understanding of John and Margaret's movements in the 1800s, although some gaps had to be imagined. These include the Little Schoolhouse & Museum in South Baymouth, the Michael's Bay Historical Society, the Bruce County Museum and Cultural Centre, the Wiarton Branch of the Bruce County Public Library, the Mayholme Foundation Genealogical and Historical Research Centre, the Grey Roots Museum and Archives, and the Archives of Ontario. Access to primary sources through Ancestry.ca was invaluable as were texts, including *Exploring Manitoulin* by Shelley J. Pearen and *History of the County of Bruce* by Norman Robertson.

Finally, I want to extend my deepest love and gratitude to my late Uncle Clive, who encouraged and supported my writing-self and helped build my connection to Manitoulin, my late brother, Tim, who is so deeply missed, my sister, Carey, my cousin and aunt, Caitlin and Linda Chisholm, my mom, Laura, whose beautiful painting graces this cover and tells a story in itself, and to the generation who will carry these stories forward: Mitchell, Jake, Finn, and Ry. And, of course, to Jason, soulmate, helpmate, husband, who has been with me through the writing of all of these words.

Historiography of Christianity in India